CONFESSIONS OF A CATHOLIC CHILD

by Elizabeth Appell

Confessions of a Catholic Child

by Elizabeth Appell
Copyright © 2016 by Elizabeth Appell

All rights reserved.

Published by EXIT PRESS.

Confessions of a Catholic Child was first produced by the Virtual Theatre Project in Los Angeles, California in August 2007.

Book design by Richard Livingston and C. White.

CAUTION: Professionals and amateurs are hereby warned that this play is subject to a royalty. It is fully protected under the copyright laws of the United States of America, and of all countries covered by the International Copyright Union (including the Dominion of Canada and the rest of the British Commonwealth), and of all countries with which the United States has reciprocal copyright relations. All rights, including professional, amateur, motion picture, recitation, lecturing, public reading, radio broadcasting, television, and the rights of translation into foreign languages, are strictly reserved.

For performance inquiries, contact Elizabeth Appell (alwaysappell@gmail.com)

For additional information about
EXIT PRESS, go to
www.exitpress.org

Paperback ISBN: 978-1-941704-11-0

EXIT PRESS
156 Eddy Street
San Francisco, CA 94102-2708
mail@theexit.org

First Edition: June 2016

Dedication

to

Will Dunne

award-winning playwright, mentor, and friend

Playwright's Statement

When a writer sets out on the journey to write a short story, a novel, a screenplay or a play there is usually something very personal at the heart of the narrative. It initially shows up as a very tiny flame, so small it's barely seen or felt. But it's there. If the writer keeps fanning it, it finally ignites into a full-fledged burn.

There are two reasons that *Confessions of a Catholic Child* caught fire. There were moments when I was young my disillusionment with the Church almost burned me to a crisp. And as long back as I can remember I've been obsessed with death.

Once Regina, the smart-mouth protagonist in *Confessions* entered the play, she freed me to dig deep into my anger at the priests and nuns that indoctrinated me with so much dread that my ten year-old soul almost withered, and she also allowed me to explore, again, my angst about my fear of death.

Almost all of my work feels the heat of this one flame: I am going to die. And then always my fear asks the big question: what happens next?

Premiere Information

The world premiere of *Confessions of a Catholic Child* was held August 18-September 23, 2007 in Los Angeles, California, produced by the Virtual Theatre Project.

Producers: Kim Terrell and Shawn Emery Ross
Director: Lauren McCormack

Cast:

Regina	Sandra Lafferty*
Kate	Heidi Mages
Spirit	Kimberly Atkinson
Announcer	Michael Vincent Carrera*
Young Woman	Megan McNulty*
Child	Megan McNulty*
Mother	Heidi Mages
Daddy	Michael Vincent Carrera*
Man	Ian Vogt*
Pope	Paul Stroili
Boy	Ian Vogt*
William	Paul Stroili

*Actors Equity Association

Set Design by John Deleonardis
Sound Design by Warren Davis
Scenic Painting by Monica Guzowski
Lighting Design by Scott Legrand
Costume Design by J.J. Pyle
Graphic Design by Actorgraphics
Publicity by Long Pine Communications
House Manager: Kimberly Van Luin
Stage Manager and Set Dresser: Julie Simpson

San Francisco Performance

The San Francisco, California performance of *Confessions of a Catholic Child* was held June 17-July 9, 2016, at the EXIT Theatre.

Producers: The EXIT Theatre
Director: Ariel Craft

Cast:

Regina	Christina Augello
Kate	Hilda Roe
Spirit	Mikka Bonel
Announcer	Stuart Bousel
Young Woman	Nic A. Sommerfeld
Child	Janice Rumschlag
Mother	Laurel Scotland-Stewart
Daddy	John Simpson
Man	Paul Rodrigues
Pope	Stuart Bousel
Boy	Nic A. Sommerfeld
William	Ron Talbot

Sound Design: Ryan Lee Short
Set Design: Amanda Ortmayer
Lighting Design: Amanda Ortmayer
Costume Design: Kitty Torres
Stage Manager: Jane Troja
Publicity: Ariel Craft

CONFESSIONS OF A CATHOLIC CHILD

by

Elizabeth Appell

Cast of Characters*

REGINA, 70ish
SPIRIT, Mid thirties
KATE, Regina's daughter, mid forties
ANNOUNCER
YOUNG WOMAN, Early twenties
CHILD, 10
MAN, Early forties, handsome
DADDY, Late fifties
MOTHER, Mid fifties
BOY, Teen-ager
POPE
WILLIAM, Early forties

Scene: The play takes place in the living room on the last night of Regina Fredrickson's life.

Time: Present

*According to need, some actors may play more than one part

ACT ONE

SETTING: The set is a combination of realistic props mixed with units (scrims are suggested) which create a mysterious effect for entrances and exits of the hallucinations. Serving as touchstones for reality include an overstuffed chair, a large couch on which a blanket is thrown over the back, a coffee table, a side-table holding a glass and a bottle of bourbon, a dressing table and a lamp. The show "Jeopardy" chatters on a television which is understood to be in the room though not actually on stage.

REGINA FREDRICKSON, sickly and agitated, wears an old chenille bathrobe and hums "Together" from the musical "Gypsy." She shuffles around trying to find a hiding place for a second bottle of bourbon. Finally she puts the bottle on the dressing table and plops a wig over it. A cigarette bobs from her mouth. Pain hits in her lower back. She looks around, pulls another bottle of bourbon from under the couch where she finds an old box. She blows off the dust, opens the lid, and pulls out a pile of pictures, a crystal rosary and her First Communion Prayer Book. As she reads from the little book she swigs from the bottle.

KATE *(from off stage):* Yoooo-hoooo…is the birthday girl home?

REGINA quickly screws the cap back on the bottle and shoves it back under the couch. Unnoticed, the pictures fall onto the floor.

KATE, an impeccably dressed executive, strides in speaking into a cell phone. A purse is slung over one shoulder and she carries one red rose and a plastic bag filled with cartons of Chinese food in the other. She casts about for a place to put the flower, but doesn't find one, so she snaps the stem and drops the flower into her mother's bourbon glass. She mutes the television.

KATE: *(into cell phone)* I told you it had to be my signature on the contract. Right. Yes. Got it? Good.

KATE claps the phone shut, drops it into her purse.

KATE: There she is. Happy Birthday, Regina. Seventy-something. You're approaching maven status.

REGINA fishes the flower out of her drink.

REGINA: A waste of good bourbon. Send flowers to my grave. Cancel that. No grave. I'm going to be stuffed. I'll make a very fine hat rack. Prop me in a corner. Katie, what are you hiding behind your back?

KATE whips a small box out from behind her back and presents it to her mother.

REGINA: For me? You want a drink?

KATE shakes her head "no." REGINA pours herself a drink.

KATE: You should stop smoking and drinking.

REGINA: Ha. That's like saying I'll never go pee-pee again.

KATE: They say it's never too late.

REGINA: A little bad news doesn't change bad habits.

REGINA unwraps the gift, opens the box.

REGINA: Diamond earrings.

KATE: Do you like them?

REGINA: Lovely, Katie. Damn good paste.

KATE: What bad news?

REGINA: They're divine, but…where will I wear them?

KATE: How about on your ears. Here, let me help you.

REGINA: When I'm wearing this old rag?

KATE tries to clip one of the earrings on REGINA's ear. The old lady bats at her daughter.

REGINA: Get away. Don't fuss over me.

Slightly wounded, KATE pulls Chinese cartons out of the plastic bag. She finds the photographs on the floor.

KATE: What're these?

REGINA: Nothing.

KATE: Who took these pictures of you?

REGINA grabs them from her, stuffs them into the album, slams it shut, sits on it.

REGINA: Nobody. Be a good girl and get us some forks. I hate eating with these sticks. Makes me feel like a primitive.

KATE exits to kitchen.

REGINA: I had an appointment with Doc Parkinson today. He's becoming a coot. His eyes have lost their shine and his mouth constantly nibbles. Does my mouth work, Kate?

KATE: *(Off stage)* And how.

REGINA: I mean like a coot's.

KATE's cell phone rings in her purse.

REGINA: Kate, your purse is ringing.

KATE enters with forks, plates, and napkins. She grabs her telephone.

KATE: Yes. Yes. What?

While KATE is on the phone, REGINA straightens her daughter's collar and smooths her hair. KATE fends off REGINA.

KATE: No, absolutely not. That's not how it should read. I told you. I thought we had it nailed. When I left the office we had it…what?…I know…what?…shit.

REGINA raises her glass to her daughter before taking a drink.

KATE: No, that won't work. No. No. I'm on my way.

KATE struggles to put her jacket on and heads for the door. A pain grabs REGINA in her lower back as she climbs out of the couch to follow KATE.

REGINA: Katie, you've haven't had a bite.

KATE: Sorry, Regina. We'll have to pick up where we left off.

REGINA: Katie, could you do me a favor and call me mommy? Just once.

KATE: Got to go. Happy Birthday. See you soon.

REGINA: Thanks for the earrings.

KATE: Wear them in good health.

REGINA: Katie.

KATE: I've got to run.

REGINA: Kate, do you ever pray?

KATE: Only on younger men. Oh, Regina, I meant to ask. What was that appointment with the doctor about?

REGINA: It was because I…I…it was nothing. Nothing. Come back tomorrow, Kate. We need to talk.

KATE goes to kiss her mother, but REGINA grabs KATE by her wrist.

REGINA: I had a dream. Last night. I dreamed…I dreamed I was planting bulbs. It was cold and gray and I was digging holes like little graves in straight lines. But it was the wrong time of year. I was placing these gnarly little things in ground at the wrong time. No, that's not right.

KATE: I've got to go.

REGINA: I'm telling it wrong. They weren't gnarly, they were—

REGINA breaks into a painful cough.

REGINA: They were smooth and pink like babies. Perfect little babies.

KATE: Perfect.

REGINA: Yes, beautiful and happy. Perfect.

KATE: Unlike me.

REGINA: Kate.

KATE: See you.

KATE unwinds from her mother, gives her an air kiss, and exits.

REGINA: That girl. I can never do it right.

From behind the scrims is a shadow and we hear a voice humming "Together" from "Gypsy."

REGINA pulls a bottle of blue medicine from a drawer in the dressing table, administers herself a spoonful. She follows it up with a slug of bourbon. With rosary in hand, a cigarette hanging out of her mouth, she falls heavily to her knees.

REGINA: Hail Mary, full of…full of…grace, the Lord is with thee, blessed art thou among women and…and…Goddamn it, I can't remember the Goddamn prayer. Blessed art thou among women and…among women and blessed is the fruit of thy womb, Jesus. That's it. Holy Mary, Mother of God…Mother of God, Mother of God, blessed is the womb. No. Blessed is the fruit. Shit.

REGINA struggles to get off her knees, falls into the couch. With a remote she turns on "Jeopardy," lights the cigarette, and pours herself a bourbon.

SPIRIT from behind the scrims sings "Together."

REGINA looks around. Sees nothing. Pours herself another slug of bourbon.

SPIRIT from behind the scrims, the song escalates.

REGINA is attacked by another brutal pain. She takes another spoonful of the blue morphine.

Lights up behind the scrim. A figure steps out from behind the scrim, a younger woman, a character we will refer to as SPIRIT, early thirties, somehow resembling REGINA and dressed as a "Prom Queen," wearing a strapless dress with full skirts, a tiara, and a pearl necklace around her neck. Her humming gives way to enthusiastic singing.

SPIRIT: (*Singing*) Where ever I go, I know she goes, where ever I go, I know she goes, no fix, no fights, no fuse and no egos…amigos… together…

REGINA: You've got it wrong.

SPIRIT: (*Singing*) Where ever you go, what ever we do, we're gonna to do it together—

REGINA: It's not fix, it's fits and it's not fuse, it's feuds…(*Beat*) Who the hell—

SPIRIT: Don't you recognize me? It hasn't been that long.

REGINA: Hail Mary, full of grace the Lord is with thee, blessed art thou among women and…and blessed is the fruit— (*REGINA peers at SPIRIT*) No, no…couldn't be…blessed is the fruit of…of thy womb… there is something about you.

SPIRIT: Of course there's something about me.

REGINA peers at the woman and crosses herself.

REGINA: I don't remember being pretty.

SPIRIT: No?

REGINA: You're quite pretty

SPIRIT: Aren't we just.

REGINA: What's that thing on your head?

SPIRIT: It's a tiara. Don't you remember?

REGINA: Remember?

Colored lights and music come up on another place on the stage.

ANNOUNCER'S VOICE: "Please welcome, Regina Fredrickson, 1949 homecoming queen."

SPIRIT giggles and whirls into the colored lights.

SPIRIT: Thank you. Thank you everyone who voted for me.

REGINA: That was over fifty years ago.

Colored lights down.

SPIRIT: Homecoming was the best night of my life.

REGINA: Goody for you. This is the last night of mine.

SPIRIT: That's exactly why I'm here. I know you are considering—

REGINA: Bumping myself off, taking myself for a long ride off a short pier? Going through the door?

SPIRIT: My, my, haven't we gotten old and bitter. What's this?

> *SPIRIT pulls an X-ray from behind the cushion and holds it up to the light, turning it in different directions trying to decipher it.*

REGINA: That's not for public consumption.

SPIRIT: I'm not public. Hmm. What's with the glamour shot?

REGINA: If you must know, it's my pancreas. Resembles Irish lace. (*Beat*) Can you see my soul?

SPIRIT: What makes you think you have one?

REGINA: I was born Catholic, Queenie. It's part of the package.

> *REGINA takes the X-ray from SPIRIT, points to it.*

REGINA: Here, a nasty little spot, and here, over here, there… everywhere…it's everywhere…we've got cancer.

SPIRIT: Come on Regina, let's dance. You can lead.

REGINA: I'll never dance again.

SPIRIT: Don't you love the way the crown catches the light? (*She sings*) Here she comes, Miss America.

REGINA: You're a slut. Always was, always will be.

SPIRIT: Define slut.

> *Lights up on YOUNG WOMAN behind the scrims. She hums the children's song, "Make New Friends, Keep the Old."*

REGINA: A woman who sleeps with ten men by her third year of marriage.

SPIRIT: That's not a slut. That's a woman with highly developed managerial skills.

REGINA: That's a slut.

> *REGINA takes another look at the X-ray.*

SPIRIT: That's a woman who really knows the meaning of networking. Besides darling, you've always been given to exaggeration. There was only one. (*SPIRIT sings*) Here she comes, Miss America…

REGINA: Hail Mary, full of grace, the Lords is with thee—

SPIRIT: I guess you took up with God after the…what shall we call it… the incident?

REGINA: Hail Mary, full of grace, the—

SPIRIT: Are we in a state of denial, darling?

REGINA: A state of grace. Go away. I have things to do and don't call me darling.

SPIRIT: Regina, what do you think of the dress? Don't you love the way the material moves?

SPIRIT pours REGINA another bourbon.

REGINA: Hail Mary full of grace, the Lord is—

SPIRIT: I don't think we've prayed since the divorce. Poor William.

REGINA: Poor William, my ass. He went after everything in a skirt. Good thing he never went to Scotland.

SPIRIT: You never understood. He tried to tell you. But you...you never listen to anybody.

REGINA: He left.

SPIRIT: You threw him out.

REGINA: He left with her and he took the silver. Arg. Enough. Let's get this over with.

REGINA takes a swig of morphine.

SPIRIT: What's the blue stuff?

REGINA: Morphine. And now for a little—

She grabs for the bourbon. SPIRIT stops her.

SPIRIT: Forget it. You're mixing a lethal cocktail.

From behind a scrim YOUNG WOMAN softly sings over the dialog until she enters.

YOUNG WOMAN: Make new friends, but keep the old, some are silver and some are gold.

SPIRIT: If you think I'm going to let you—

REGINA: It's my prerogative. We're only helping things along. You want to play the lingering game? Happy little moments that include wet diapers and pain so agonizing you see lights. We're toast. There will be no miracles for us, kiddo.

SPIRIT: If we can be elected homecoming queen, anything's possible. (*Singing*) Here she comes, Miss America. Is Bert Parks still alive?

YOUNG WOMAN steps out from behind the scrim.

YOUNG WOMAN: Mommy.

REGINA: Who in the hell is that?

SPIRIT: A regret?

YOUNG WOMAN: Mommy.

SPIRIT: She reminds me of somebody. Who is it, darling?

REGINA: Can the darling stuff. Where's my remote? I'm missing *Jeopardy*.

SPIRIT: Welcome to our returning champion, the Young Woman who last week won over five thousand dollars. Tonight the categories are Abortion, Abortion, and Abortion. What category do you want?

YOUNG WOMAN: I'll take Abortion for two hundred.

SPIRIT: What small town mother took a lover and ended the resulting pregnancy?

> *Buzzer blasts.*

YOUNG WOMAN: Regina Fredrickson.

SPIRIT: Correct.

> *Applause. YOUNG WOMAN claps excitedly. Caught up, SPIRIT whirls.*

REGINA: Wait just a damn minute.

YOUNG WOMAN: I'll take Abortion for five hundred.

SPIRIT: What Catholic woman ended a pregnancy and never sought forgiveness in confession?

> *Buzzer blasts.*

YOUNG WOMAN: Who is Regina Fredrickson?

SPIRIT: You are correct for five hundred dollars.

> *Applause. SPIRIT and YOUNG WOMAN whirl in excitement.*

REGINA: What are you saying? I never—

YOUNG WOMAN: I'll take Abortion for a thousand.

REGINA: No you won't. I never, never had an abor…an abor…I never did anything like that. You don't know me very well.

YOUNG WOMAN: I belong to you.

REGINA: Oh, my God. I need a drink. Where's my crossword?

> *REGINA finds the puzzle on the table. Picks it up.*

REGINA: What's an adjective made up of nine letters that means threatening or virulent?

YOUNG WOMAN: I would have been a good girl. I would have loved you.

REGINA: Don't bother me unless you know the word.

> *SPIRIT dances around REGINA singing "Together."*

YOUNG WOMAN leans close and kisses REGINA. As she does, she lifts REGINA's rosary. SPIRIT sees her. YOUNG WOMAN heads for the scrim.

SPIRIT: Hey. Hey, you.

REGINA: Leave her alone. Let her go. I've got enough to worry about.

SPIRIT: But she took your—

REGINA: Can it, Queenie.

YOUNG WOMAN exits behind the scrim. She disappears as lights fade on her.

REGINA: It wasn't something I wanted to do.

SPIRIT: (*Giggling*) But you did it.

REGINA: Shut your mouth. Smugly accusing me. Who do you think you are?

SPIRIT: Queen. Homecoming Queen.

REGINA: Look, I don't want to be rude, but get the hell out of here.

SPIRIT: What's the rush?

REGINA: I've got things to do before I…go through the door.

SPIRIT: Like what?

REGINA: Like cancel the newspaper, check the will, clean the bathroom, finish the puzzle.

REGINA fills in the puzzle.

REGINA: M-a-l-i-g-n-a-n-t. She was right. That works.

SPIRIT: No, Regina. There's more.

REGINA: Like what?

SPIRIT: Confession.

REGINA: Confession's for sissies.

SPIRIT: And Communion.

REGINA: Maybe.

SPIRIT: Ah, ha. The Last Rites.

REGINA: Do they carry a lifetime guarantee?

REGINA hobbles to her closet.

REGINA: What do you think? Should I be found in the black dress?

SPIRIT: Cut too low. When you lie on your back, your breasts disappear. You'll look like a corpse in drag.

REGINA: How about the green one?

SPIRIT: Matches your skin.

REGINA: The pink one?

SPIRIT: No, no. Too pedestrian. None of these. I know. We have to go shopping for just the right dress.

REGINA: The black one's fine. The black's divine.

SPIRIT: Regina, you do this and we'll go to hell.

REGINA: That has occurred to me.

SPIRIT: Eternal damnation.

REGINA: Couldn't be worse than what I'm going through now.

SPIRIT: Offing yourself is definitely against the rules.

REGINA: Maybe I'll reconsider confession. After all, it is one of the perks of being Catholic.

SPIRIT: I repeat, against the rules. Besides, you can't go through the door until you've got your ducks in a row.

REGINA: What ducks?

SPIRIT: You're ducks, darling.

REGINA: Don't call me darling.

SPIRIT: Come on, Regina. Put your feet up. Take a load off. All this is very anxiety producing and highly stressful for—

REGINA: What ducks?

SPIRIT: Duck ducks.

REGINA: Be specific.

SPIRIT: You know. Quacky little things.

SPIRIT waddles and quacks.

REGINA: Like what? Like what?

SPIRIT: God, Regina, you got a cathode ray tube connected to your spinal chord? (*Beat*) Okay. Ducks. Like making amends. Like saying you're sorry for the things you've done to the people in your life. And the sumo duck of them all.

SPIRIT stands on a chair.

SPIRIT: The daddy duck, the grande-mundo duck-a-roo…you must forgive yourself.

REGINA: Oh, those ducks.

SPIRIT mimes dancing with a partner.

SPIRIT: I'd love to dance. Thank you. No one's every called me angel eyes before.

REGINA: Stop that. Sit down. You might have a point. I don't want to go with sin on my soul.

SPIRIT: She's getting it. By golly, she's getting it. When you pass through that door, you want to be as spotless as a virgin's under panties.

REGINA: What do you know about under panties…you don't wear any.

A pain grabs REGINA.

REGINA: I know what you're doing. You're trying to get me off track. Let me tell you, fluff head, I don't give a flying duck about forgiveness. I'm going and I'm going tonight.

SPIRIT: Oh, sure, you wizened bag of cancer, easy for you to do, because never, I repeat never in your life have you examined one moment of your poor pathetic existence.

REGINA: Let me tell you something, you with a wind tunnel for a brain. Whether I examined or didn't examine, whether I lived or was never born makes not one pea pie bit of difference…to anyone.

REGINA shakily administers herself a teaspoon of morphine.

SPIRIT: What about burning in hell?

REGINA: What about it?

SPIRIT: These skirts. They're flammable.

REGINA: You're the one who survives, for crying out loud. Isn't that what they tell us? The spirit survives.

SPIRIT: In hell?

REGINA: No, no. You turn into breath, enter another soul…and start over.

SPIRIT: How do you know that?

REGINA: I don't. I just made it up. (*Beat*) I want to be laid out like in *The Godfather*, holding my rosary.

SPIRIT: I just want to be laid.

REGINA: This is my death. Butt out. In the name of the Father, and of the Son and of the—

SPIRIT: The worst thing that can be said about a person is that she did not pay attention.

REGINA's hit by another pain.

REGINA: Crap. This is all crap.

SPIRIT: Don't do this. At least not tonight. Not until you've got your ducks…all your ducks in a row.

> *REGINA is hit by pain. She falls onto the couch. SPIRIT raises her feet and covers her with a blanket then she curls up at the other end.*

REGINA: I want to go…I want to go.

SPIRIT: Not yet, old girl. Not yet.

> *REGINA picks up her First Holy Communion Prayer Book from the table and thumbs through it. REGINA falls asleep.*
>
> *Gregorian chant. Lights up on a ten year old girl dressed for First Holy Communion. She carries a crystal rosary. REGINA looks unbelieving at the girl.*
>
> *NOTE: Every time CHILD says the name of "Jesus," she dramatically bows her head.*

CHILD: By making my first Holy Communion, I become the Bride of Christ. In other words, I'm going to be Mrs. J. C. I'm going to be Jesus's bride and I'm going to be pure in thought, word, and deed. I'll still go to confession because nobody's perfect, but I won't really have to.

REGINA: Oh, my God.

> *REGINA nudges SPIRIT with her foot and awakens her.*

SPIRIT: (*Yawning*) Hey, kid, nice dress.

CHILD: I'll write beautiful poems and stories for my husband, Jesus. I'll make Jell-O pudding for him. I'll always have bubble gum whenever he wants it and I'll laugh when he makes jokes.

SPIRIT: The beginning.

REGINA: The what?

SPIRIT: I think she's the beginning.

REGINA: Pure, innocent…a pretty little thing, wasn't I?

SPIRIT: In a perverse sort of way.

CHILD: I'm going to suffer.

REGINA: She's got that right. (*To SPIRIT*) I'm not up to this. Do me a favor and tell her to get the hell out of here.

SPIRIT: (*To CHILD*) Get the hell out of here.

REGINA: Not like that.

CHILD: I'm going to suffer for my husband because he died for me on the cross.

REGINA: (*To SPIRIT*) You're worthless. (*To CHILD*) Listen you silly little girl.

> *REGINA lights a cigarette.*

REGINA: Dreams don't come true.

CHILD: Don't say that. My dreams will come true.

REGINA: The part about suffering for your husband…that part will come true.

SPIRIT: Don't be so hard on her.

> *SPIRIT gets off the couch, does some stretching.*

CHILD: Then I'm right? I will marry Jesus? Cool.

REGINA: Not Jesus, you drip.

CHILD: You should bow your head when you say "Jesus."

SPIRIT: That rings a bell.

REGINA: Jesus, Shemesus. This may come as a shock to you little girl, but it's just the way it is. I hate you.

SPIRIT: Here we go.

CHILD: Jesus says to hate someone is a venial sin. (*She sings*) Jesus loves me, This I know, 'Cause the Bible tells me so, Little children dah dah dah…I forget it…They are weak, dah dah dah dah…

REGINA: Don't sing Protestant hymns.

SPIRIT: She's adorable.

CHILD: (*At the top of her lungs*) Yes Jesus loves me, Yes Jesus loves me…

REGINA: Shut your mouth. You'll land you in Purgatory.

CHILD: (*Sings these line quickly*) Yes Jesus loves me, The Bible tells me so. Well he does. (*Beat*) Why do you hate me?

REGINA: You grew up…that's reason enough.

> *REGINA pours herself a shot of bourbon. Knocks it back.*

REGINA: You grew up and…and nothing…you just…exist.

SPIRIT: She means she feels guilty for not doing more with her—

REGINA: I mean I hate her. This is none of your business. Go polish your crown.

> *SPIRIT takes to the couch.*

CHILD: Sister Julie Delores tells me Jesus loves me and he is my shepherd.

REGINA: That makes you a stupid little sheep.

CHILD: Sister says Jesus is my protector and my loving shepherd.

REGINA: Shepherds fleece their lambs.

CHILD: Sister says my shepherd, Jesus, died for me.

REGINA: Shepherds take their lambs to market to be slaughtered.

CHILD: (*Tearfully*) Jesus wouldn't let that happen to me. Jesus loves me, I tell you. Jesus loves me.

REGINA: Stop bobbing your head like it's hinged.

CHILD: Sister says that's what I'm suppose to do.

REGINA: What you're suppose to do is grow up to be an extraordinary woman, marry an extraordinary man, have extraordinary children—

CHILD: What's…extra…ordinary?

REGINA: It's ordinary, but with an…extra…serving of…ordinary.

CHILD: Then I don't want to be extraordinary. I'm going to grow up to be…special.

REGINA: But you didn't turn out special, did you? You just grew up.

CHILD: I don't know…yet. I'm just…ten. It's my birthday.

REGINA: Bully for you.

CHILD: I will write great plays…and I will learn to love Jesus with my whole heart and soul.

REGINA: Did you do that?

SPIRIT: Oh, oh, I don't think so.

CHILD: I don't know. I'm still a little girl.

REGINA: Can you keep a secret little girl?

CHILD: Yes. Except from Jesus. Jesus knows everything.

REGINA: Stop that infernal bobbing. (*Beat*) The secrets I'm going to tell you even God doesn't know.

CHILD: How can that be?

REGINA: God gave us a will, did he not?

SPIRIT: Regina, it's not polite to ask those kinds of questions.

REGINA: (*To SPIRIT*) Why? Afraid of the answers? (*To CHILD*) Well? Did God give us a will?

CHILD: A will to choose from good and evil.

REGINA: And does God know whether you're going to choose good… or evil…before you make the choice?

SPIRIT: Oh, Lord.

CHILD: I…I think…I think God knows if—

REGINA: Of course he doesn't know. That's one of the secrets. It's your will. He's not making the choice. Isn't that true?

CHILD: Golly…I…I'm not—

REGINA: True or false?

CHILD: I…I…don't know what to—

REGINA: True or false?

CHILD: I'm a little confused.

REGINA: Of course you are. That's part of God's divine plan.

CHILD: Don't you love God?

SPIRIT: Careful, old girl.

REGINA: (*To CHILD*) You little snip. Of course I love God.

CHILD: You're so…so…mean.

REGINA: I'm not mean. Just a little toughened…around the edges… it comes when your time runs out. You see…I just…I just wanted you to grow up and—

CHILD: I will. I promise.

REGINA: I wanted you to grow up and—

CHILD: I've got a stomachache in my throat.

REGINA: I wanted you to grow up and make your life count.

CHILD: I'm cold.

REGINA: Jump up and down. Get your blood moving.

SPIRIT: I think she wants you to—

REGINA: (*To SPIRIT*) I know what she wants. (*To CHILD*) Little girl, these secrets aren't that painful. Enough of this. Go away. I'm busy. Newspaper cancelled, bathroom cleaned. I need to finish my puzzle.

> *REGINA grabs the unfinished crossword puzzle, puts her glasses on and tries to concentrate on it.*

SPIRIT: Can't you just give the kid a hug.

> *REGINA takes off her glasses.*

REGINA: Listen, you. Take your tiara and those ridiculous skirts and flounce your twitchy little butt back to where you came from.

The CHILD reaches out, but REGINA rebuffs her.

CHILD: You're so mad at me…and mad at God, too.

An image of the bourbon bottle glows brightly on the scrim.

REGINA: Shhhh. That's one of the secrets.

REGINA is gripped by terrible pain. The CHILD gives her a spoonful of morphine.

CHILD: I love secrets.

Lights down on CHILD. REGINA puts on her glasses, studies the puzzle.

REGINA: What's a seven letter word that's a noun meaning hara-kari?

Lights up on MOTHER and DADDY in the bourbon bottle. Both speak from inside the bottle.

MOTHER: Seppuku.

REGINA: S-e-p-u-k-u?

MOTHER: You always were a lousy speller, Regina. S-e-p-P-u-k-u. Does that finish the puzzle?

REGINA: Almost.

MOTHER: Finish what you begin, Regina. Always finish what you begin.

DADDY: Regina, I want to talk to you.

SPIRIT: They look so old. They're not my parents. Never saw them before in my life.

REGINA: (*To SPIRIT*) Lying doesn't change who your parents are. (*To MOTHER*) What's a ten letter word meaning the formal remission of sin imparted by a priest?

MOTHER: That's an easy one, Regina. You shouldn't have to ask me. Absolution. A-b-s-o-l-u-t-i-o-n.

DADDY: Regina, I want to talk to you. Daughter, I need you to do something for me.

REGINA: Daddy, I thought you and Mother had…had…

MOTHER: Can you get us a drink, dear?

REGINA: My stomach hurts.

MOTHER: It's your birthday, kiddo. Your stomach always hurts on your birthday.

DADDY: Happy Birthday, dear.

REGINA: This is…confusing. I thought you both went…through the door.

MOTHER: What door? What door is she talking about Daddy?

REGINA: I'm dying. Did you know that?

MOTHER: That's good, dear. What about the drink?

DADDY: Say "please," Mother. That's how we taught Regina. Please can you get us a drink?

REGINA: I've got cancer.

DADDY: Could you…this is probably asking a lot, but…could you get us out of here?

REGINA: God, how many times did I beg you to get out?

MOTHER: No point in crying over spilled milk. But better than spilled bourbon, I always say.

MOTHER laughs at her joke.

MOTHER: Be a good girl and get us something to—

REGINA: I'm bone dry.

SPIRIT: Regina, let them go. It's too late. There's nothing they can do for you.

REGINA: (*To SPIRIT*) Is there nothing I do where your nose doesn't go?

SPIRIT: (*Singing*) Where ever you go, what ever you do, we're going to do it together.

MOTHER: There's always another bottle, dear…somewhere.

DADDY: Relax, Mother. Regina's going to get us out of here.

MOTHER: What? You've got to be crazy. I'm not leaving. Nobody can pry me out of here.

DADDY: You obstinate old woman. She can get us out.

MOTHER: I don't care what you say, Daddy. I'm not leaving here.

DADDY: If I leave, you go with me, Mother. You hear me?

MOTHER: Squeeze me down to the size of a swizzle stick and you still won't get me out.

DADDY: She's a bit in her cups, Regina. You know the signs.

REGINA: Lord knows. We're so much alike. Talk to me Mother. Tell me about going through the door. Were you frightened when you—

MOTHER: Are you wearing clean underwear, Regina? Should, you know. Always wear clean underwear in case of an automobile accident.

REGINA: She's impossible. My mother's impossible. I can't talk to her. Never could.

SPIRIT: Come on, Regina, let's go cut a rug.

REGINA: Mother, I don't have much time.

MOTHER: Regina, your posture. Stand up straight.

REGINA and SPIRIT adjust their posture.

SPIRIT: This is all a waste.

REGINA: (*To SPIRIT*) Would you can it? I've had it with you.

REGINA grabs SPIRIT by the shoulders and shakes her until the tiara falls off.

REGINA: Every time I open my mouth you're here muddying up the water.

SPIRIT: Let go of me or I'll call the police.

REGINA: Go ahead. You'll end up in a padded cell.

SPIRIT: I only tell the truth.

SPIRIT retrieves her tiara.

REGINA: What do you know about the truth? You spent most of your life telling yourself lies. Daddy?

DADDY: Yes, daughter.

REGINA: Daddy, I need something from you.

DADDY: Of course, Regina. What can this lonely old man do for you?

REGINA: Lonely? Are you lonely?

DADDY: No, not exactly lonely. That's not the right word. Limited is closer to the truth.

MOTHER: Regina, please. Just a little taste.

REGINA: I'm not getting you a drink and I'm not getting you out of the bottle.

DADDY: Why, Regina?

MOTHER: Nothing's changed. Get us a drink, Regina.

DADDY: Hush, Mother. That's no way to deal with Regina. Tell Daddy what you need, Regina.

MOTHER: She's a spiteful, sinful girl, Daddy.

DADDY: What is it, dear?

Long beat.

REGINA: I want you to apologize.

DADDY: I couldn't hear you, Regina. I'm a little deaf in my left ear. Speak up, dear.

REGINA: Apologize to me.

DADDY: For what, daughter?

MOTHER: She's manipulating you, Daddy.

DADDY: (*To MOTHER*) Shhhhhh. (*To REGINA*) For what, Regina?

REGINA: For the painful…the awful—

MOTHER: She doesn't even know.

REGINA: Oh I know. Do you remember that night, and I was sitting in the living room with my boy friend?

SPIRIT: Must you open every wound?

DADDY: Joe?

MOTHER: (*Flirtatious*) Who could forget Joe?

REGINA: The night of the Sadie Hawkins dance. I made him a blue shirt to match his eyes. And you…you…

MOTHER: You're slouching, Regina. Pull in your stomach.

REGINA and SPIRIT pull in their stomachs.

SPIRIT: So much truth.

REGINA: (*To SPIRIT*) You're the one who told me to get my ducks in a row.

SPIRIT: This one's no duck. This one's a turkey.

REGINA: Remember, Daddy. You came down the stairs.

DADDY: I came down the stairs?

REGINA: Yes, yes, you came down the stairs. Into the room.

DADDY: I came down the stairs into the room.

MOTHER: Don't listen to her, Daddy. You know how Regina gets.

SPIRIT: Regina, don't do this.

REGINA: You came down the stairs drunk.

SPIRIT: No. Don't.

REGINA: Drunk and naked.

Long silence.

MOTHER: It's not true. She's telling a story. (*Beat*) It's a story, isn't it, Daddy?

DADDY: Regina…I—

REGINA snatches the bourbon bottle from off the side table, turns her back on her parents, and shakily drinks.

MOTHER: Anger is a sin, Regina. So is greed. Regina, who made you?

REGINA: (*In a small voice*) God made me.

MOTHER: And what is the Sixth Commandment, Regina?

REGINA: Honor thy father and thy mother?

MOTHER: Precisely. Share that bourbon with Daddy and Mommy.

REGINA: Living in that bottle is a sin. Look at you…condemned.

MOTHER: We are not condemned, Regina. Whatever gave you that idea?

DADDY: I don't think I…I don't think I did what you…well…all that, so long ago. So long. And now, now you've become an edgy woman, Regina. Get us out of here and we'll talk.

REGINA: You think I'm a stupid, gullible ten year-old? My Daddy wants me to be his savior.

Lights up on MAN, early forties, drop-dead handsome. He's wearing black, sports a photographer's vest and carries a camera and tripod. He sets up the tripod for shooting.

DADDY: Please, Regina. Let us out.

MOTHER: Don't beg her, Daddy. Don't lower yourself. Regina, dear, what's a seven letter word across meaning voluntary intercourse between a married person and a partner other than the lawful spouse?

MOTHER disappears.

REGINA: A-d-u-l-t-a-r-y?

DADDY: E-r-y, I believe. E-r-y, Regina. My dear girl, about our request—

REGINA: What about mine?

DADDY: I always did my best.

Lights down on DADDY.

MAN: Hold that look.

The MAN takes a shot of REGINA.

MAN: That's the look I want to photograph…vulnerable, confused.

Startled at first, REGINA peers at him, then a look of recognition overcomes her. She pinches her cheeks, wets her lips and smiles.

REGINA nudges SPIRIT.

REGINA: Hey, Queenie. Look over there. One of our secrets.

SPIRIT: What are you babbling about?

REGINA: That man. All the bulges in the right place.

SPIRIT: Hmm? Oh, my God, Regina. It's him.

REGINA: Uh huh.

SPIRIT: The photographer.

REGINA: Somehow…he looks like…like a priest.

MAN: Raise your chin, just a bit, Regina. (*REGINA raises her chin.*) Good. Just a little more.

SPIRIT: Jesus, Mary, Joseph.

REGINA: Wait. Stop. I don't want to do this.

SPIRIT: That's not what you said then.

REGINA: Let me tell you, you self-indulgent, shallow, over-sexed, and under-trained little—

SPIRIT: Under-trained?

REGINA: You heard me.

The photographer gets off shots of the two women.

SPIRIT: Under-trained for what?

REGINA: For being a human being.

SPIRIT strikes poses for the photographer.

SPIRIT: I left that job to you.

REGINA: For being a woman.

SPIRIT: A beautiful, sexual woman.

REGINA: Yes…no.

SPIRIT: An affectionate, passionate woman.

REGINA: A good woman.

SPIRIT: A woman who slipped from the straight and narrow.

REGINA: That wasn't me. That was you.

SPIRIT: Uh, oh. He's coming over.

REGINA: I'm mistaken. I don't know him. Never seen him before. Tell him to go away. He's dangerous.

SPIRIT: Ah, ha. How would you know if you don't remember him?

REGINA: He swaggers. A man who swaggers is dangerous. Get rid of him.

SPIRIT: I will not.

REGINA: You will. And now.

SPIRIT: Okay, okay. You want me to talk to him? You got it.

SPIRIT breathes into her hand and smells her breath.

SPIRIT: My breath fresh? Watch, baby girl. Watch carefully.

SPIRIT tentatively approaches MAN. Dance music lilts in the background.

MAN: (*To SPIRIT*) Hello. Dance?

SPIRIT melts at the sight of this dreamboat and reaches out her hand to him. Simultaneously REGINA reaches her hand out to him. The MAN leads SPIRIT down stage and into his arms.

MAN: You're a beautiful woman.

REGINA: Psssst. Careful. Careful.

SPIRIT: (*To REGINA*) Remember, Regina. I think it went something like this. (*To MAN*) Please…don't do this.

MAN: You're a beautiful, lonely woman.

SPIRIT: (*To REGINA*) Remember being lonely? (*To the MAN*) I've never been lonely a day in my life.

MAN: It shows in your eyes…the loneliness.

REGINA: He saw it in my eyes?

SPIRIT: (*To REGINA*) Yes, he saw it in your eyes. (*To MAN*) Being a woman is sometimes a lonely thing…usually it's a secret loneliness…maybe that's what you see. My husband, William, is a good man, but together we create…distances…he wants…you know…things…well, it's…it's complicated.

MAN: I want to crawl inside of you…become you.

REGINA: What a line.

SPIRIT: No. No, no. (*Beat*) Maybe.

REGINA: I said that?

MAN: You want me inside of you.

REGINA: He read me like a book.

MAN: My heart aches…or is it yours I feel?

REGINA: I can't breathe.

SPIRIT: I can't breathe.

MAN: Our falling together is an act of nature.

REGINA: He was always saying things like that.

SPIRIT: Remember, Regina. I can't…I mustn't…

SPIRIT attempts a feeble escape, but MAN gently catches her and holds her face in his hands.

MAN: You won't regret this.

REGINA: Don't listen to him. He's beautiful, but you're heading for a heartbreak.

The MAN pulls SPIRIT toward him. She resists but finally succumbs and they kiss very tentatively, then hungrily. Suddenly SPIRIT pulls back, looks frantically for REGINA.

SPIRIT: Did you see?

REGINA: I see I made it so damn easy for him.

MAN: (*To SPIRIT*) Don't move.

Quickly he moves back to the tripod and gets off some shots of SPIRIT posing.

REGINA: I've forgotten how free I felt with him.

MAN: Come here you gorgeous creature.

The MAN chases SPIRIT. She giggles with delight. He catches her. They fall onto the couch laughing, kissing and cooing.

MAN: This is our special place.

SPIRIT: Our cheesy little motel with the L broken off the sign.

REGINA: Our mote.

MAN: It's our mote. Our very own mote.

REGINA: He made me laugh.

SPIRIT: (*To REGINA*) Remember. You slept with your leg draped over his.

REGINA: Only once.

SPIRIT: Come on, Regina.

REGINA: Twice…

SPIRIT: This is not the time to…

REGINA: All right, all right…we did it. We did it a lot…but we loved each other.

MAN: Tell me. Tell me you love me.

SPIRIT touches his face, leans forward.

SPIRIT: God, forgive me.

SPIRIT kisses him passionately, then pulls away and walks to another part of stage.

REGINA: (*To SPIRIT*) You had no choice.

SPIRIT: Don't tell me. Tell him.

MAN: (*To REGINA*) Why did you leave me? Just like that. One day here. Next day gone.

SPIRIT: Go on. Tell him.

REGINA: It's just a story.

MAN: Come here. Please.

REGINA slowly joins him. He wraps his arms around her and she relaxes into him. She sighs deeply.

MAN: What's that dribble of blue on your lips? (*He leans down and kisses her lips.*) Umm. Morphine. Great stuff.

The MAN holds REGINA. SPIRIT leans against the MAN's back. The three sway together.

SPIRIT: Go on, Regina. Tell him.

REGINA: Yes. The story. I want to tell you.

MAN: Whisper it in my ear.

REGINA: It's not that kind of story.

MAN: Come closer, Regina.

REGINA: It's about the…oh, God, oh, God…it's about the pregnancy.

The three stop dead. A long beat and then they separate.

MAN: I dreamed about it.

REGINA: You dreamed about it?

REGINA rushes to him, pulls a clerical collar from her robe pocket and places it around his neck causing him to take on the image of a priest. REGINA grabs at him as she falls to her knees.

REGINA: Bless me, Father, I confess, this is my last confession and these are my sins.

MAN: I can't forgive you, my sweet. Only you can do that.

REGINA: But you're a priest.

SPIRIT: Regina wants her lover to be her priest.

MAN: You don't really buy that rubbish, Regina? Do you think a man can stand for God?

SPIRIT: Yeah, Regina. Do you think a man can stand for God?

The MAN moves to the camera, prepares to set up a shot.

SPIRIT: Tell him you're sorry.

REGINA: Now?

SPIRIT: Tell him.

REGINA: I can't.

SPIRIT: Why can't you?

REGINA: (*Silence*)

SPIRIT: Regina?

REGINA: Because I'm not.

SPIRIT smiles, embraces REGINA.

MAN: That's great. Hold it.

REGINA pulls away.

REGINA: I'm a good woman…a good woman and I believe in—

SPIRIT: George Burns. He played God. She believes in George Burns.

REGINA: I go to Mass on Sundays.

SPIRIT: You haven't gone for years.

REGINA: I make the Stations of the Cross.

SPIRIT: The only stations you made were train stations.

REGINA: I say my Rosary.

SPIRIT: You can't remember the words.

MAN: Cut yourself some slack, Regina. Stand over there. I want to take another picture.

REGINA: Oh, no…my hair, my make-up. I'm a mess.

MAN: You're beautiful.

SPIRIT: Hear that, Regina?

REGINA is hit by agonizing pain.

REGINA: I need a drink.

Lights down on MAN. Lights up on POPE, a man in long white robes wearing a beanie. He carries a silver tray on which is a bottle of bourbon and two shot glasses.

POPE: (*In a Gregorian sounding chant*) Ask and ye shall receive.

The POPE hands REGINA and SPIRIT each a shot glass.

REGINA: I'll be Goddamned.

SPIRIT: He looks like the Pope.

POPE: You got that right, ladies. The one and only.

REGINA: Forgive my mouth your Holiness…it's just…well…we…we're a little surprised that you're…well, that you're…

POPE: Rarely things are what you think they are.

The POPE pours REGINA and SPIRIT a drink and then swigs out of the bottle.

POPE: Here's to alcoholism, martyrism, catechism…Catholicism.

They clink glasses and knock back the bourbon.

REGINA: I don't want to disappoint you, your Holiness, but I'm afraid I've strayed from the flock. I probably fall into the classification of…of…

POPE: Infidel? An interesting phenomenon…infidelity. Fills the churches with desperate, insecure, guilt-ridden people. Absolutely delightful.

REGINA: Forgive me, Holy Father, for all the bad things I've done in my life.

POPE: How about the good things you didn't do?

REGINA: Those too.

SPIRIT: So, Mr. Pope…you going to let her off the hook?

POPE: (*To REGINA*) Want to kiss my ring?

SPIRIT: Don't kiss it. Beg your pardon, your Highness…

REGINA: (*In a loud whisper*) Your Holiness…your Holiness. Why shouldn't I kiss it?

SPIRIT: It's unsanitary.

POPE: No problem. (*The POPE attempts to spray the ring with Lysol but the can doesn't work.*). Goes to show you, the only thing you can depend on is the devil.

The POPE thinks he's very funny. Almost in a swoon, REGINA kisses the ring.

POPE: I love this part.

The POPE gives them each a refill, but when he takes a nip for himself, the bottle is empty.

POPE: Dash it all. Seems I'm fresh out of booze.

SPIRIT: No problem, your Popeness.

REGINA gives her a kick.

SPIRIT: Ouch…your Highness.

REGINA gives her another kick.

SPIRIT: Your Holiness. There's always another bottle somewhere.

SPIRIT pulls the bottle from under the wig. Opens it, hands it to the POPE.

POPE: Aged?

SPIRIT: Older than Regina, your Beanieship.

The POPE pours them another drink. They clink their glasses against the bottle. They all drink.

POPE: Here's to bourbon, a great calmer of pain and concealer of truth.

SPIRIT and the POPE clink glass and bottle .

POPE: Our girl, Regina here, she's an expert in numbing the truth, aren't you, Regina.

REGINA: Well, I do my best, your Holiness. I always do my best.

POPE: That's right, Regina…when it comes to avoidance…you're the best, the master of the fleet, the top of the heap, the cream of the crop.

REGINA: You've hit the nail on the head. She's about to get out of this world and not face the music, if you get my drift.

POPE: You mean you're going to commit suicide?

REGINA: No, no, I wouldn't do that. I wouldn't do such a sinful, terrible—

POPE: Here's to suicide.

The POPE raises the bottle and takes a drink.

POPE: As long as it's tidy.

REGINA: But isn't it a mortal sin? A very big mortal sin?

POPE: I look on it as a form of sacrifice. Take Jesus, for example. He hung around, er…bad choice of words. What I mean he could have taken off at any time and left those old boys to their own devices.

REGINA: Oh, dear, nothing's prepared me for this. I'm so confused.

SPIRIT: Part of the divine plan.

The POPE gives them each another drink. The three of them are getting tight.

POPE: Regina, what do you believe you must do to go to heaven?

At the word "heaven," he sings and does a brief soft shoe.

POPE: Heaven, I'm in heaven, and my heart beats so that I can hardly speak—

SPIRIT: (*Giggling*) She believes she'll go to heaven because she's a Catholic.

POPE: (*Belly laugh*) Rome's public relations is fabulous, isn't? Better than anything Washington comes out with.

REGINA: Lately a little lapsed.

SPIRIT: Heavily lapsed.

REGINA: That may be, but I haven't lost my faith. I mean I was born—

SPIRIT: A Catholic.

REGINA: (*To POPE*) My faith is always there—

SPIRIT: When I need it.

POPE: My faith is always there when I need it...in a Swiss bank.

The three of them thinks this is a riot.

SPIRIT: Would you like to dance?

REGINA: How dare you speak to the Pontiff that way.

SPIRIT: Give the guy a break. He's only human.

POPE: I'd love to dance.

Charleston music comes up. The POPE breaks into the dance. SPIRIT joins him, but REGINA is annoyed.

POPE: I enjoy any kind of heavy breathing I can get.

SPIRIT: Tell me your Majesty, I'm curious. Are you really into all this Catholic crap...or...or are you on a humongous power trip?

POPE: I have to confess...I love the pope-mobile. That sucker can get up to a hundred miles an hour on the straight away.

SPIRIT: Cool.

REGINA: Hail Mary full of grace, the Lord is with thee. See your Holiness, I haven't forgotten one word. Hail Mary full of grace, the Lord is with...ah...with...Hail Mary... full of...full of...why the hell can't I remember?

SPIRIT: She's a little rusty. Long time between rosaries.

REGINA: Your Holiness, I've been thinking.

POPE: That's bad for my business. Thinking is very bad for Catholicism.

REGINA: Yes, well, it occurs to me that you have quite a lot of pull. If I should do this thing, you know. If I take the long walk off a short pier—

POPE: You mean commit suicide?

REGINA: Ah…well…yes, ah, if I were to commit sui…ah…if I were to do it. Could you forgive me now? I mean before I do it so I won't go to… to—

POPE: To hell?

REGINA: Precisely. Could I have absolution in advance?

The POPE takes a swig.

POPE: Sure, no problem.

He raises the bottle and toasts her.

POPE: You're absolute. There. You have it.

REGINA: I don't think you understand. I want you to—

POPE: You want me to what, Regina? Wipe the board clean?

REGINA: Isn't that what you're suppose to—

POPE: Okay, okay. I can do that.

The POPE mimes wiping a board.

POPE: There. Feel better?

REGINA: I thought I would—

POPE: Feel peaceful and free?

REGINA: All my life I've been taught that—

POPE: Regina, Regina. The most profound—

The POPE pours them each another drink, takes one for himself.

POPE: The most profound, personal transformations…ah, those words, so…so pontifical. Anyway, the personal transformations come only when you are ready. So, my dear, Regina. Are you ready?

SPIRIT: Be careful, Regina.

REGINA: Yes, your Holiness.

POPE: Are you sure, because what I'm going to tell you is one of the great secrets to life.

SPIRIT: She's a terrible listener, but I'm all ears, my sensors are tuned, my aerial reaching high into the sky, my antenna beamed toward—

REGINA: Can it, Queenie. I'm ready.

Long beat.

POPE: You must take…responsibility.

REGINA: Responsibility?

POPE: Yes, yes. I pray every day asking for the boys at the Vatican to do likewise.

REGINA: That's it?

POPE: Another touch?

The POPE pours another drink for SPIRIT. REGINA refuses.

REGINA: Are you sure? I mean are you absolutely, unequivocally sure?

POPE: Girly, girl, I know that's tougher than a shot of bourbon to swallow.

REGINA: Wait just a god damn minute. You've been scamming me.

POPE: Ah, a light glimmers, an illumination, a beam of radiant energy filters through—

REGINA: All my life I've been taught to seek forgiveness from Father Pat or Father Michael, Monsignor Horrigan…always needing some Goddamn man to absolve me.

POPE: Yes, yes, but now you know. Now you know—

The POPE motions for her to finish his sentence.

REGINA: Now I know what?

POPE: You know that it's up to you.

REGINA: You mean…what you're saying is…I can…I can forgive myself?

SPIRIT: No, no, that's not what he means. (*To POPE*) Is it?

POPE: She got it. Hallelujah. Oops. Suppose that sounds a little Baptist.

REGINA: Do you understand what this means, Queenie? I'm free. I'm free.

REGINA does a little dance.

REGINA: Do you realize? It means I'm in control. Whoopee.

SPIRIT: Oh, dear.

REGINA: I can breathe again. I feel marvelous. Better than I've felt for years. Bring on the sarcoma, carcinoma, melanoma. Bring on the corruption, the torment, anguish, and pain. Bring on the decay. I'm free. (*Beat*) So, Queenie, what do you think?

SPIRIT: What you're saying, Your Popeness, if she does this thing, she won't necessarily burn in the fires of hell forever?

POPE: That's what I'm saying. For that matter, nor will you.

REGINA: Free, free, free.

SPIRIT: What do you mean? What do I have to do with this?

POPE: One thing I know for sure. Whatever you decide, you're going to have to do it together. I've seen it work both ways. (*To REGINA*) I've seen it when you go first and she follows. (*To SPIRIT*) And I've seen it when you go first and she follows. I've never seen it when one goes and the other stays.

SPIRIT: You mean, where ever she goes, I go?

POPE: (*He raises the bottle*) Here's to revelation. There's another nifty pontifical word.

SPIRIT: This is not fair.

REGINA: (*Sings*) Where ever we go, what ever we do, we're gonna go through it together. Through thick and through thin, all out and all in, we're gonna do it together…

A bell chimes. He cocks an ear.

POPE: I'm being paged.

SPIRIT: Your Popeness, wait.

POPE: One for the road.

He takes a last swig and caps the bottle.

POPE: So. My advice is. If you're so hell-bent, excuse my Latin, to do this, the two of you better get your act together.

A second bell.

POPE: Ring-a-ding-ding.

The POPE collects the glasses and the bottle and puts them back onto the tray, blesses them. He turns to leave, but REGINA gracefully retrieves her bottle of bourbon.

SPIRIT: I don't want to go.

REGINA: We're going tonight, Queenie.

Lights up on MAN and his camera. The POPE puts down the tray, puts REGINA under one arm, SPIRIT under the other and faces them toward the photographer.

SPIRIT: Nooooo.

REGINA: We're going through the door…tonight.

SPIRIT: Not this kid. You'll never get this kid through the door.

REGINA: Tonight.
MAN: Smile, ladies. (*Flash.*)

BLACKOUT.

INTERMISSION

ACT TWO

REGINA sleeps on the couch. "Jeopardy" chatters in the background. SPIRIT reclines on the back of the sofa watching the show. KATE enters with a huge bouquet of flowers in a vase. She plunks them down on top of the TV. REGINA awakens, evaluates the flowers, gets up and moves them to the floor. KATE moves the flowers back. REGINA puts them on the floor. KATE begins to move them again.

REGINA: Don't touch those flowers.

KATE: They look better up on the—

REGINA: Don't touch them.

KATE: You don't like them.

REGINA: I like them.

KATE: No you don't. I can tell. You don't like them.

REGINA: I like them.

KATE: I know you, Regina…you don't—

REGINA: (*To SPIRIT*) Aren't they nice?

SPIRIT: Yes, darling, they're very nice.

KATE: If you liked them, you'd—

REGINA: I like them. They're beautiful, wonderful. They're the floweriest flowers that have ever flowered. I like them. What are you doing here? What time is it? (*Looks at her watch*) Ten. It's after ten. Two visits in one night…and flowers…big flowers.

KATE: Can we turn that damn thing down?

KATE doesn't notice that SPIRIT makes her magic and turns down the TV.

KATE: I called the doctor.

REGINA: What'd you call him?

KATE: No matter what I do, I can't please you.

A circle of colored lights come on one side of the stage and music plays, "Wake Up Little Susie."

REGINA: You're so damn angry. What have I ever done to you?

KATE picks up one of the yellowed photographs. REGINA snatches it out of her hand and plunges it into her bathrobe pocket.

KATE: You're right. What have you ever done to me?

A teen-age BOY enters colored lights.

KATE: You don't remember. How could you? You were always…always in your cups, feeling no pain. I hated the way—

REGINA: You don't know what you're talking about.

As KATE moves into the light she pulls her hair up into a pony tail, casts off the executive jacket and removes the long skirt to expose a shorter one transforming her into a teen-ager. She folds into the BOY's arms. They dance cheek to cheek.

SPIRIT: Go on. Go over. You might find a duck or two.

REGINA: A duck?

SPIRIT: You might learn something.

REGINA: The past is God's lethal weapon.

REGINA takes a drink and moves into the light. Her speech is slightly slurred, her step, unsteady.

REGINA: My, the evening is lovely. Reminds me of when I was a girl.

KATE: Mommy, you promised you'd stay inside the house.

REGINA: When I was your age we used to have parties out on Slaughter House Road…in an old barn. Colored lights…live music…my English teacher played the saxophone…those syrupy notes hung like colored lights in the hot summer night.

KATE: Mommy.

REGINA: Sometimes the boys would fight. We formed circles around them. "Get him, Charlie. Look out, Jack." Everybody screamed and yelled. I think I screamed. I doubt I've screamed since.

KATE leaves the BOY to try and coax REGINA out of the circle of light.

KATE: The *Honeymooners* are on. You're missing Ralph and Trixie.

REGINA moves toward KATE's boyfriend, forcing herself into his arms. Awkward and embarrassed, the BOY dances with her.

REGINA: Put both your arms around me.

The BOY looks to KATE for help.

REGINA: That's right. Remember how we danced? Our bodies close and damp.

BOY: You're quite a dancer, Mrs. Fredrickson.

REGINA: Call me, Regina.

BOY: You're quite a dancer, Regina.

REGINA: I love to dance.

KATE: Go back into the house…please.

REGINA: Young man, hold me closer. Be confident…make it easy for me to follow you.

KATE: You're making a fool of yourself.

REGINA caresses the BOY's face.

REGINA: You're strong. What's your name?

BOY: Mrs. Fredrickson…gee…seems like I should be dancing with—

KATE: Mother.

BOY: Golly, I…

REGINA: You have a name?

KATE: Regina, please.

BOY: My name's Robert.

REGINA: You like dancing with me, Robert?

BOY: Yeah…Mrs. Fredrickson…great, great…but, I think I should get back to…

REGINA: You're very athletic, aren't you, Robert?

KATE: Go in. Go into the house.

REGINA: I like all of Katie's friends.

KATE: Regina.

REGINA: Very athletic.

KATE angrily exits to the couch where she assumes her adult self.

REGINA: Now what's bothering my Kate? I never seem to please that girl, know what I mean?

REGINA turns to leave, but comes back to the BOY.

REGINA: You're a good dancer. What'd you say your name is?

BOY is silent.

REGINA: It doesn't matter. You're a very good dancer.

Lights down on BOY. REGINA frantically looks around for KATE. She exits the lights and joins KATE on the couch.

REGINA: The memories, Kate. I'm drowning in them.

KATE: Hold your breath.

REGINA: That time I danced with one of your boyfriends. You got all hot and bothered.

KATE: A long time ago. The things you would do.

REGINA: I meant nothing by it…nothing.

KATE: Are you in pain?

REGINA: Maybe it was the lights that night, or the heat. It was an unusually hot summer.

KATE: The doc said you should get a lot of rest.

REGINA: I probably had a couple of cocktails…it meant nothing, but now I can see how you—

KATE: I don't want to talk about it.

Fatigued, KATE curls in the overstuffed chair and stretches.

KATE: God, I'm exhausted. This job, it's draining me.

REGINA: We have to talk.

KATE yawns.

REGINA: I don't want to leave you without—

KATE: (*Sleepily*) It's too late. Too late. What's done is done. The doctor said you need to take it easy.

KATE falls asleep.

REGINA: Now I can see. That night…that night you thought…thought I was…oh, God, from the moment you were born and I held you in my arms wet and squalling, I only wanted perfection for you. Only perfection.

REGINA covers KATE with the throw, then she sits on the couch and proceeds to make notes.

SPIRIT: Seems melodramatic to me. Offing yourself.

REGINA: Doesn't matter if you think it's melodramatic. What matters is if I think it's melodramatic and I don't. So. Go on about your business. I have things to do.

SPIRIT: You are my business.

REGINA: Huh. You're on a short-term assignment, kiddo.

SPIRIT: We should plan a vacation, a holiday, you know, something to look forward to.

REGINA: Way too busy. I'm planning my funeral. Got to write the eulogy. Hate the way they lie about dead people. Don't want any fuss. Pine box. For music I want a nice little up-beat Gregorian chant. Let's see. What's left on my list? Tweak will. Done. Pay bills. Done. Clean bathroom. Done. Cancel newspaper. Oh, shit. Still have to cancel *People*

Magazine, finish my cross-word puzzle, write down memorial invitees. Won't be much of a turnout. Most of my friends are dead.

SPIRIT: Regina, stop this.

REGINA: Be sure Kate gets the buffet menu. No prawns. I hate those little pink things. Look like fetuses with whiskers.

SPIRIT: You're not really going to do this.

REGINA: Wrong, Queenie. I am. I really am.

SPIRIT: You want to go through that door?

REGINA: It's like this, dearie, we go through doors every day. We get up in the morning and make the decision to have Special K over Cherios and we go through a door. We meet a man and don't marry him and we go through a door. We meet another man and marry him and we go through a door. We're going through doors all the time. What's the big deal about his one?

SPIRIT: Well, for one thing, once it closes, you can't get back in.

REGINA: You know that for sure?

SPIRIT: You don't know what's behind it. Might be the IRS or a dentist's office…or…or…

REGINA: Or nothing. Just blessed peace.

SPIRIT: Regina, you do this and we'll go to hell.

REGINA: Where do you think we are right now? *(Beat)* Besides, remember what his Holiness…

SPIRIT: Forget him. He was tighter than two coats of paint.

REGINA: Queenie, stop worrying. It's just a matter of letting go. We just have to let go.

REGINA lights a cigarette. SPIRIT grabs it and stubs it out.

REGINA: Let go and let our grimy little souls fly. Now, where's my rosary? You take my rosary?

SPIRIT: Interesting how the whole religious thing kicks in when we think we're on the way out.

REGINA: This is my death. I'll do it anyway I wish.

SPIRIT: So. How about before we go through the door we plan a little getaway to Hawaii or Mexico. How about Paris?

REGINA's grabbed by pain.

REGINA: Get over here. Now.

REGINA takes a spoonful of morphine.

SPIRIT: You can't make me. You're not my boss.

REGINA: Get over here and get ready.

REGINA grabs SPIRIT and wrestles her to the couch. A lively physical battle ensues.

REGINA: Lie down and act like you're dying.

SPIRIT: Get away from me. Let me up. Let me up.

SPIRIT's tiara falls off.

SPIRIT: My tiara.

REGINA: This is hard enough without you acting like a crazy woman.

The SPIRIT fights back.

SPIRIT: I don't mind getting fucked on this couch but I don't want to die on it.

REGINA: What's the difference?

SPIRIT: With one you can make believe it didn't happen, with the other you can't.

Straddling SPIRIT, an equal contender, with all her might REGINA holds her down.

SPIRIT: You're afraid to live.

REGINA: You're afraid to die. Say it. You're afraid to die.

SPIRIT: You're afraid to die.

REGINA: No, you twit, say, I'm afraid to die.

SPIRIT: But you're not.

REGINA: I know I'm not. You are. Say it.

SPIRIT: Say what?

REGINA: Oh my God, you're hopeless. Not only hopeless…you're useless.

Totally spent REGINA collapses onto the couch. Both women take a beat to catch their breath.

SPIRIT: Where's my tiara?

REGINA: Who cares about that stupid crown?

SPIRIT: May I remind you, your world would have fallen apart, I mean shattered into a zillion pieces if you hadn't been elected Homecoming Queen.

REGINA is silent. SPIRIT searches for her crown, finds it, and examines it. She wails.

SPIRIT: It's not real.

REGINA: It's real paste.

> *SPIRIT wails.*

SPIRIT: I want a real one with real jewels.

REGINA: We don't always get what we want.

> *Exhausted REGINA takes to the couch. SPIRIT covers her with the throw blanket. REGINA desperately grabs at SPIRIT.*

REGINA: I want to go…and I want you to go with me.

SPIRIT: Never.

REGINA: You…don't…have…a…choice. Don't you understand? Fight me and we'll go in a painful rage. Join me and we'll tap dance our way through.

SPIRIT: I don't know how to tap dance. I always wanted to take lessons, but you were so tied to that damn couch, you wouldn't…

REGINA: The tap dancing thing was a metaphor, for God's sake.

SPIRIT: Can't we hold off just a little while?

REGINA: No. Absolutely not. Now. Where's my rosary?

SPIRIT: Here use these.

> *SPIRIT takes the pearl necklace off and tries to hand it to REGINA. Angrily REGINA rejects it.*

REGINA: I want my rosary.

> *SPIRIT pushes the necklace at REGINA who takes it.*

REGINA: William gave me these pearls for my birthday years ago. I thought they were beautiful then. Still do.

WILLIAM: *(From the darkness)* Did you know I wanted to kill you?

> *REGINA cocks an ear.*

WILLIAM: *(From the darkness)* Shoot, strangle, or poison. It really didn't matter to me.

SPIRIT: William?

> *Lights up on WILLIAM sitting on a garden bench. REGINA pretends she doesn't see him.*

REGINA: What's left to do? The eulogy.

SPIRIT: It's William.

REGINA: Impossible.

SPIRIT: Oh, Lord.

WILLIAM: Strangling you seemed appropriate and the most satisfying.

REGINA: That man. I loved and hated him at the same time. (*Beat*) He was desperately hurt when he discovered you were—

SPIRIT: Having the affair? He never knew.

REGINA: He knew, he knew. Don't you remember? The night I found him in the garden? His anger was paralyzing.

WILLIAM: I wanted to see you dead.

REGINA: Stick around.

She nudges SPIRIT.

REGINA: Go talk to him.

SPIRIT: You talk to him. This is your gig.

WILLIAM: I yearned to see you laid out cold for all eternity.

REGINA: I've gotten so old, he won't recognize me.

SPIRIT tries to leave, but WILLIAM grabs her by the arm.

SPIRIT: (*To REGINA*) Don't leave me alone with him.

WILLIAM: Why did you leave me? Just walked out. I even know the date, because it was your birthday.

SPIRIT: I left you?

WILLIAM: We need to talk. We never talked…and then when I—

SPIRIT: Okay, okay, Buster Brown. You want to talk? We'll talk. Shall we begin with the topic of your women? Since the day we were married you—

WILLIAM: I looked but I never touched.

REGINA: Don't let him get away with that. Remember the twit from the café?

SPIRIT: How about the twit from the café?

WILLIAM: I never touched her.

REGINA: (*To SPIRIT*) Remember the way his eyes would—

WILLIAM: You were so beautiful. You drove me wild.

REGINA: Brother, it was a short trip.

WILLIAM: You never looked at me. Always past me…through me.

SPIRIT: I was afraid.

WILLIAM: (*To SPIRIT*) Afraid of what?

REGINA: Of what she might see.

SPIRIT: I didn't understand why—

WILLIAM: You didn't understand what?

SPIRIT: Why you left with her.

REGINA: And you took the silver.

SPIRIT: And you took the silver.

WILLIAM: She meant nothing to me. You were the one I loved.

REGINA/SPIRT: My mother's silver.

WILLIAM: The girl…she was just…a test…kind of…like a test…I just needed to know if—

REGINA/SPIRIT: Settings for twelve.

WILLIAM: It was me, Regina. Something was wrong with me.

REGINA: The demitasse spoons, the butter knives, the soup ladle.

WILLIAM: Don't you remember? Don't you remember us…in bed…I couldn't seem to—

SPIRIT: I don't remember. (*To REGINA*) If we don't remember things, do they count?

REGINA: (*To SPIRIT*) Tell him to give it back, at least the demitasse.

SPIRIT: Give them back. The years. I want them back.

WILLIAM: I hated myself…hated my—

SPIRIT: That was my fault?

REGINA: It was all her fault, wasn't it? Everything was always her fault. The moon wasn't full. Regina's fault. Spring sprang late. Regina's fault. The love making was not so—

WILLIAM: I felt…helpless.

REGINA: That was her fault too?

WILLIAM: I never had the courage to say the things I needed to say.

SPIRIT: All those other women.

REGINA: Wait. Ask him. What things did he want to say?

REGINA/SPIRIT: I can't breathe.

WILLIAM: There were no others. (*Beat*) I understood why you spent time with that other man.

SPIRIT: You knew?

A pain hits REGINA.

SPIRIT: All that time I thought it was me. I thought you weren't attracted to—

WILLIAM: At first, when you left, I wanted to die.

SPIRIT: You desired me?

WILLIAM: I thought I couldn't survive not having you.

SPIRIT: You desired me?

WILLIAM: I was so angry you had taken the possibilities away from us. Furious. I wanted to hang you by your beautiful neck. But little by little I understood.

SPIRIT: And then the accident.

WILLIAM: After you left, I was never with another woman.

SPIRIT: That awful night, Kate came over to tell me. I couldn't believe you were—

WILLIAM: A blaze of lights and a crack…of…of…glass.

SPIRIT: At first I thought Kate was being her perverse self, her dark ironic—

WILLIAM: Rolling over and over, the world upside down, right side up, slashing, crashing, metal buckling and folding into me.

SPIRIT: Then you were gone.

WILLIAM: So much unsaid.

REGINA: Afterwards, came the nightmares.

WILLIAM: The last thing I said to you before the crash: I hope you die.

The MAN enters. Aims his camera. Flash.

MAN: Now lovebirds. Let's get a shot up close and personal.

REGINA: William…I…I…

SPIRIT shrinks from the camera.

MAN: (*To REGINA and WILLIAM*) Oh, come on you two. Ham it up a little. Say cheese.

WILLIAM: Regina, I want to tell you—

MAN: One more. Everybody…cheese. (*Flash*)

SPIRIT: If you weren't…you know…if you could have, would it have changed anything?

WILLIAM: I loved you.

MAN: So, you with the crown on your head, how do you reply to that?

SPIRIT smiles shyly and poses for the photographer.

REGINA: William…William…maybe I was…maybe I…I misunderstood.

SPIRIT: Yes. I misunderstood.

WILLIAM: A lifetime of speaking different languages.

REGINA: I want to ask you, William…I wonder…could you possibly… I'm dying, William. I need your…forgiveness.

WILLIAM touches REGINA's face. Her hand covers his.

WILLIAM: Forgiveness is something you get in confession. Love is what I can give you and you've always had that.

REGINA: Oh, God…I'm sorry…I'm so very sorry.

Lights down on all except the MAN. Lights up on the bourbon bottle.

MAN: I love the confessions. They're the best part. But they never really solve anything. I mean if I go into the darkroom and try and erase a mistake on the film, does it work? No. I end up changing the meaning of the picture.

He raises his hand and blesses the audience.

MAN: In nominee Patris, et Filee, et Spirito Sancti. Amen.

MOTHER and DADDY appear in the bourbon bottle.

MOTHER: The last word in the puzzle. Did you get it, Regina?

REGINA: Four letters across starting with C. An adult male chicken, a hat tilting or jauntily turning upward.

MOTHER: Come on, Regina. You know it. Think. The vulgar slang word for a man's—

REGINA: Got it. Got it. Puzzle's done. I'm finished.

MOTHER: Regina, darling. Who's your friend?

REGINA: Mother, do you ever think about forgiveness?

MOTHER: Been drinking, Regina? Shame on you. You don't look well. A little peaked. Are you taking your vitamin C?

DADDY: Mother, where have you been? I've been looking everywhere for you.

SPIRIT: I feel terrible. Must have a hangover. I'd give my seat in hell for an aspirin.

MOTHER: (*To MAN*) Youuhooo, you with the nice, long lens. Know how to do the Bossa Nova?

SPIRIT: He knows how to do everything.

DADDY: Mother, you saggy-breasted sot. You think he'd be interested in you?

The next eight speeches are spoken to REGINA simultaneously and they gradually rise in volume.

MOTHER: Regina, if you don't want him. I'll take him.

DADDY: Regina, don't pay any attention to her.

SPIRIT: Get that guy out of here, Regina. I don't want him taking my picture.

MAN: You're all afraid to look at the truth.

WILLIAM: You didn't understand. I loved you.

MOTHER: Get us a drink, Regina.

DADDY: Get us out of the bottle, Regina.

WILLIAM: Love is what I can give you.

REGINA: Quiet.

Silence. REGINA gathers her wits.

REGINA: Out of here. Everyone. (*She points to the MAN*) That includes you and take your long lens with you.

The MAN grabs one more shot. Flash.

BLACKOUT.

Lights up on REGINA, smoking, going over a list. SPIRIT sits on the back of the couch. KATE awakens in the chair, stretches, moves the flowers from floor to the TV. One look from REGINA and KATE moves them back to the floor.

REGINA: You had a little snooze. Better go home, Katie and get a proper night's sleep.

KATE: What time is it?

REGINA: Little after midnight.

KATE: Regina, the doctor said—

REGINA: I can tell by the look on your face. He gave you the gory details, and you believe every last one of them.

KATE nods.

REGINA: Where's the remote? Time for *Wheel of Fortune* reruns. The best thing about that show is Vanna's wardrobe changes. They're positively miraculous.

KATE: Regina, this is your life.

REGINA: Thank you Ralph Edwards.

SPIRIT: I loved that show.

KATE: Are you in pain?

REGINA: Only when I laugh.

SPIRIT: Bitterness, how sweet it is.

SPIRIT does some stretches.

REGINA: (*To SPIRIT*) I didn't ask you to this party.

KATE assumes REGINA is speaking to her.

KATE: If I don't come over here I feel shitty. If I do come…I feel shitty. How do you do this to me?

REGINA: I have a gift.

KATE: First thing tomorrow we're going to get a second opinion.

SPIRIT: Yes, yes.

REGINA: I've put myself into God's hands.

KATE: He's got butter fingers.

REGINA: God would never drop me.

KATE: Right through the cracks.

REGINA: Do you think so?

KATE: Oh, shit, what am I saying? No, of course not. God…God will take good care of you. Yes, he will. Good care.

KATE crosses her legs.

REGINA: (*To SPIRIT*) Would you stop those stupid contortions?

Again KATE thinks REGINA is talking to her.

KATE: Crossing my legs is hardly a contortion.

SPIRIT lights on the back of the couch posing dramatically. REGINA lights a cigarette and KATE tries to take it away from her. REGINA fends her off.

REGINA: Smoking is one of my three pleasures in life.

KATE: I know. The other two are bourbon and *Jeopardy*.

REGINA: Wrong, Miss Know-It-All. The other two are having my corns removed and producing regular bowel movements.

KATE: You are an impossible old lady. (*Beat*) What's happening to me?

REGINA: Kate, isn't there a secret part of you that believes in God?

SPIRIT hisses at REGINA from the sidelines.

KATE: To hell with God.

SPIRIT recoils.

REGINA: Katie.

KATE: (*Pointing to the television*) There's your god.

REGINA: Your anger comes out of fear, Kate. Confess. It's your own death you're frightened of.

Lights up on CHILD.

KATE: Me confess. You confess. Confess you lived like a dragon, here in your lair, smoking and bristling when anyone tries to get beneath that armor of yours.

REGINA: Kate, I—

KATE: Look at you. You've smoked and drank your life away. Daddy left and you—

REGINA: No. I left him. All the other women…he would never have left me, he said so himself. He loved me.

CHILD: Now I lay me down to sleep—

KATE: I remember that he—

REGINA: I'm telling you, I'm telling you the story.

CHILD: Pray the Lord my soul to keep—

KATE: I don't know.

REGINA: After the accident—

KATE: All I know is he died, suddenly. He left me forever. Afterwards you took to the couch. And now you're leaving me.

CHILD: And if I should die before I wake—

REGINA: What do you want from me?

KATE: I want you to fight this damned disease. I want you to stay alive.

CHILD: I pray the Lord my soul to take.

SPIRIT: Bless you Katie, my girl.

REGINA: Go home, Kate. Come back when it's over.

KATE: Regina, fight. Fight this thing.

REGINA: I am…in my way.

REGINA puts up her dukes, jabs like a prize fighter.

KATE: What do you mean?

REGINA places the flowers on the television.

REGINA: Not a thing. I'm a foolish old lady whose mouth is working like a coot. Now I should rest. Just like the doctor said.

REGINA lies down on the couch.

KATE: A nap.

REGINA: Yes.

KATE: That's all you're going to do. Just...take a nap.

REGINA: That's all I'm going to do.

KATE: Nothing more. No...extraordinary acts.

REGINA: Katie, my girl, have you ever known your mother to do anything extraordinary?

KATE: Regina, promise me that you won't—

Lights up on MOTHER in the bourbon bottle.

REGINA: I promise, I promise. Run along. Thank you again for the earrings...and the beautiful flowers.

KATE: I'll see you tomorrow?

REGINA: Tomorrow?

KATE: I'll bring you the newest TV Guide. Tomorrow.

REGINA: Tomorrow. Of course, my darling.

KATE covers her mother with the throw blanket.

KATE: Good night. Sleep well.

KATE exits.

CHILD joins REGINA, crouches next to the couch.

MOTHER: Get up, Regina. Time to get ready to go to Mass.

CHILD: I love to go to Mass.

REGINA becomes age 16, lying on the couch as if it were her bed, comes to, turns her face away from her MOTHER.

REGINA: I can't go today, Mother. I don't feel well.

CHILD: I feel fine.

MOTHER: Get up. I'll drive you.

REGINA: Why?

MOTHER: Why what?

REGINA: *(Sits up)* Why should I go to Mass?

CHILD: Because if you don't go it's a mortal sin.

MOTHER: I know you're sixteen and think you have a complete and a total understanding of the workings of the universe. I've got news for you, Toots. When you're grown up and are under your own roof, then you can decide whether or not to go to Mass. Until then, you'll do as I say. Now get up and get ready for church.

CHILD: Get up.

REGINA: What does it matter if I go to church?

CHILD: If you don't, it's a mortal sin.

MOTHER: Catechism 101: It's a mortal sin to miss Mass on Sunday.

CHILD: See? I told you so.

REGINA: (*To Child*) Shut up. You're like a mosquito.

MOTHER: You'll have to go to confession.

REGINA: I'm a more interesting person with mortal sin on my soul.

MOTHER: You're making me angry, Regina. Haven't I taken on enough of you and your father's sins without having to add anger at my daughter? Get ready.

REGINA: I have a stomachache in my throat.

MOTHER: Regina, get dressed.

REGINA: Why are we Catholic?

> *CHILD makes the sign of the cross, presses her hands together and bows her head.*

MOTHER: I'll meet you at the car.

REGINA: Why?

MOTHER: Because that's your form of transportation.

REGINA: Why not a Baptist...or a Buddhist?

MOTHER: Because we don't want to go to hell.

REGINA: Why? I mean, what do you think is there?

MOTHER: Wear your new skirt.

REGINA: How can you be so sure about things you've never seen?

MOTHER: When you do what you're suppose to do, you find your faith. I go to Confession and I go to Communion and I say the Rosary and I make the Stations of the Cross and I never miss Mass and I don't eat meat on Friday...I have my faith because I was born to it and I take care of it, and you were born to it too. Get dressed.

REGINA: Want to know what I think?

MOTHER: No. Get dressed.

REGINA: I think you're scared.

MOTHER laughs as her image and the bottle fades.

Lights down on CHILD.

Lights up on dressing table. REGINA enters, sits on the stool in front of the mirror. REGINA puts on the earrings KATE gave her and applies make-up transforming herself into a vital and radiant woman.

REGINA: (*To SPIRIT*) I've got to admit, I've got the willies.

SPIRIT: You should be scared to death…or…something. (*Beat*) Why the war paint?

REGINA: I know what those funeral homes make you look like. I'll do my own, thank you very much.

SPIRIT: Go easy on the blush. The Shirley Temple look is out.

From behind the scrims.

YOUNG WOMAN: Mommy?

SPIRIT: Not too much eye shadow.

YOUNG WOMAN: Mommy.

REGINA: Oh, my Lord in heaven. Any one but her. Please, get rid of her.

YOUNG WOMAN steps out from the scrims and approaches REGINA.

SPIRIT: Me? Forget it. I'm taking a cruise on the Love Boat.

YOUNG WOMAN: Tell me the story.

REGINA: My stories are becoming confused.

YOUNG WOMAN: Please.

SPIRIT: You can't ignore her, Regina.

REGINA: (*To SPIRIT*) Get lost, prom queen. (*To YOUNG WOMAN*) Come here. Let me look at you.

SPIRIT: She's lovely.

YOUNG WOMAN: (*To REGINA*) Remember, Mommy?

REGINA turns toward SPIRIT.

REGINA: If you insist on sticking around, make yourself useful. Please, help me.

Lights up on MOTHER in the bourbon bottle.

SPIRIT: Nope. This one's your baby, so to speak. You got rid of her once. Time for you to take over.

MOTHER: (*Laughing*) No use crying over spilled bourbon.

Lights down on MOTHER.

SPIRIT: Just explain to her.

REGINA: I…I'm…not sure I can.

SPIRIT: Please. For her, for me.

REGINA: Why should I do anything for you?

SPIRIT: Because…because, deary, because we need to say the words. We have to take responsibility.

REGINA: Responsibility. Yes. Responsibility. (*To YOUNG WOMAN*) Okay, okay, I did it.

SPIRIT: Say all the words.

REGINA whirls on YOUNG WOMAN.

REGINA: All right. All right. You didn't belong to William. It was a very, very difficult situation. Do you understand what I'm saying? I didn't want to do it. I didn't mean to do it. I didn't want to do it. I had to…there was no choice.

SPIRIT: But you did it.

REGINA: I did it. I said it. Are you happy? (*Beat*) Where's the remote?

YOUNG WOMAN takes REGINA's hands in hers, forcing REGINA to look at her.

YOUNG WOMAN: Tell me…tell me where I came from.

SPIRIT puts her hands on YOUNG WOMAN's shoulders,

REGINA: Oh, God, I don't know, I don't know…I can't tell—

SPIRIT: Responsibility.

YOUNG WOMAN: Tell me.

REGINA: Well…I suppose…I suppose.

SPIRIT: One of the secrets.

REGINA: Yes. Yes. You came from…you came from love. You came from a great, warm, wet and wonderful love.

Lights up on the MAN in the priest's collar. He blesses them.

MAN: In the name of the Father and of the Son and of the Holy Ghost.

Lights down on MAN.

REGINA: I wonder if I came from love?

Lights up on DADDY in the bourbon bottle.

DADDY: I did my best. I was a good father.

Lights down on DADDY.

The YOUNG WOMAN holds out the crystal rosary to REGINA who grabs it.

REGINA: You. You took my rosary.

SPIRIT: I tried to tell you.

YOUNG WOMAN: I wanted something to remember you by.

REGINA: Didn't anyone ever tell you stealing is a sin?

SPIRIT: The Ninth Commandment. Thou shalt not steal.

REGINA: (*To SPIRIT*) Listen to you.

YOUNG WOMAN: I'm sorry, but it seemed to be such a little thing. I didn't mean to—

REGINA: Oh, dear. This is so…so…here.

REGINA hands the rosary to the YOUNG WOMAN.

REGINA: Here. Take it. (*YOUNG WOMAN hesitates.*) Take it. Please.

SPIRIT: Aren't we getting smaltzy.

REGINA: (*To YOUNG WOMAN*) Please. Take it. I want…I want you…I want you to have it.

YOUNG WOMAN is thrilled and smiles radiantly. She throws a kiss to REGINA and slowly backs away.

YOUNG WOMAN: Thank you, Mommy. (*As lights fade on YOUNG WOMAN she sings*) Make new friends, but keep the old, some are silver and some are gold.

REGINA: Don't go. Not yet…please…don't go.

REGINA stretches out on the couch.

REGINA: Oh, dear, oh, dear, oh, dear.

She crosses her arms over her chest as if she were lying in a coffin.

SPIRIT: Regina. What are you doing?

REGINA: Practicing.

SPIRIT: Practicing what?

REGINA: Practicing lying in my coffin.

SPIRIT: You're what?

REGINA: Practicing being dead.

SPIRIT: Regina, Regina. Please.

REGINA: Hmm.

SPIRIT: (*Passionately incoherent*) Please, Regina, let's not do this. It scares me just to think about it…please, I don't want to…to…do you understand…I don't think you…what I'm saying, oh, don't do this to us, the blackness, the terrible blackness…maybe forever, oh God, let's pass on this dying thing. That's it. Let's just not do it. Let's cheat and never die. Regina. Please.

> *SPIRIT tries to pull REGINA out of the pretend coffin. REGINA is dead weight.*

SPIRIT: Lord, woman, are you made of lead?

> *SPIRIT tries again, but REGINA won't budge. SPIRIT squats next to the couch, clutches at REGINA's robe.*

SPIRIT: We can find a way to get us out of this mess. We know how. After all, we've cheated our way through up until now. Never really living. Hiding, taking no risks, going for absolutely nothing. We're masters. We just have to sit down and calmly come up with a way to do it again. What do you say?

> *Long beat. REGINA slowly pries her robe out of SPIRIT's hands.*

REGINA: (*Sings slowly and softly*) Where ever I go, I know you go, where ever I go, I know we go, no fits, no fights, no feuds, and no egos… amigos…together.

SPIRIT: That's it?

> *Lights up on tall, unique door that seems to float in space.*

REGINA: That's it.

> *A tired and beaten SPIRIT climbs into the end of the couch opposite REGINA.*

REGINA: Get out of my coffin.

SPIRIT: It's my coffin too.

REGINA: Is not.

SPIRIT: Is too.

REGINA: Is not.

SPIRIT: Is too.

REGINA: Okay, stay where you are.

REGINA gets up and staggers toward the door. SPIRIT makes a dash for REGINA, forcing herself between REGINA and the door.

SPIRIT: Okay, Regina, okay, but not yet. You can't go through when you're drunk.

Lights up on CHILD.

REGINA: Plenty people do. Give me one reason why I shouldn't.

SPIRIT: Because…because…ah…you're not…not in such…close contact with God?

REGINA: Assuming there is one.

CHILD: (*Wails*) Don't say things like that.

REGINA: It's time. Be a good girl and come along peacefully.

CHILD: I am a good girl. (*To SPIRIT*) Aren't I a good girl?

SPIRIT: I have to go to the bathroom.

REGINA: So do I. You first.

SPIRIT exits to the bathroom.

SPIRIT: (*Off stage*) Uh, oh.

REGINA: Now what?

SPIRIT: (*Off stage*) Sorry, I can't go tonight. I have the runs.

REGINA: It's nerves. Don't make a mess. I've cleaned that throne until it is spotless and that's how I want it left.

SPIRIT: (*Off stage*) I can't go anywhere under these circumstances.

Toilet flushes. SPIRIT enters.

REGINA: You think you're the only one to leave a trail of shit to Death's door?

REGINA exits to the bathroom.

SPIRIT: I will not be humiliated.

REGINA: (*Off stage*) Isn't living without purpose humiliation enough?

SPIRIT: Regina. You think I have no purpose?

REGINA: (*Off stage*) Up until tonight I would have answered yes.

CHILD: Do you think I have purpose?

Toilet flushes. REGINA enters looking stunning wearing the black dress.

REGINA: I think you're pathetic. Where's the frustrated prom queen?

> *CHILD wails and points to SPIRIT who sits at the dressing table putting on make-up.*

CHILD: You think she has purpose but you don't think I do and you're going away and leaving me without saying good-by or anything and I will never know—

REGINA: Child, Child, hush. Come here.

> *REGINA sits on the couch. The CHILD sits next to her.*

REGINA: You are a difficult child to love.

CHILD: It's only because I'm so—

REGINA: I know, I know. You're so young…and so bloody needy.

CHILD: Maybe if you just took the time to get to know me.

REGINA: There's no time left.

CHILD: Tell me.

REGINA: Tell you what?

CHILD: Tell me who I am.

REGINA: You are…I don't know…you are…did you hear the secrets?

> *Lights come up on DADDY in the bottle.*

CHILD: I think so.

REGINA: You had to listen carefully.

CHILD: I didn't understand them, but I'm still good girl aren't I? Even if I don't know what they mean.

REGINA: Yes. You're a good girl. Don't worry about them. Most secrets are only interesting to the fool who tells them.

CHILD: Do you love me?

REGINA: Yes, I—

DADDY: Regina, Regina.

REGINA: It's my father, Child. I must go.

CHILD: Say you love me. Say that.

REGINA: That.

CHILD: Say…I…love…you.

REGINA: Yes. That.

SPIRIT: Regina…for god's sake.

REGINA: Oh, all right. I love you. I love you.

> *REGINA gives the CHILD a big, warm hug.*

REGINA: (*Turning to DADDY*) Do things really ever change, Daddy?

DADDY: Oh, I don't know, dear. It's not something that I'd advise you to think a lot about. Regina. Regina...I just want you to know...I just want you to know...none of this was...well, was your fault.

REGINA: Thank you. Thank you, Daddy. (*Beat*) Is Mother...is she there?

DADDY: No. I think this time she's faded for good.

REGINA: Do you think she's all right?

DADDY: I think so. It's always hard to tell with your Mother.

REGINA: We're so much alike.

DADDY: Your Mother's a good woman.

REGINA: Daddy...Daddy...forgive me, Daddy. I'm sorry, I couldn't—

DADDY: No more regrets, child. It's too late. If I run into your Mother, I'll tell her you wanted to help us. Don't be so hard on yourself. Good-by, Regina.

REGINA: No. Don't go.

CHILD: Daddy, don't go.

SPIRIT: Stay. Please.

DADDY: Take care of yourself, Regina.

REGINA: Hold me. I'm cold...and very...I'm...I'm—

CHILD: I'm a little bit afraid.

DADDY: I was never very good at things like that.

REGINA: Please.

CHILD: Daddy.

SPIRIT: Daddy.

DADDY: Good-by, my dear daughter.

> *Lights fade on DADDY in the bottle.*
>
> *Lights fade on CHILD.*
>
> *REGINA looks for a long moment at where DADDY stood, blows her nose, then busies herself getting things in order.*
>
> *KATE enters. She startles REGINA.*
>
> *The lights from now to the end of the play become deeper and deeper blue.*

REGINA: Katie. (*Looks at her watch*) It's three in the morning. You should be home.

SPIRIT: Ah, Kate. My last hope. Maybe she can convince my pal not to—

REGINA: You startled me.

KATE: Regina, thank God, you're still here.

REGINA: Of course I'm still here. Where do you think an old lady would go on a night like this?

KATE: I had a feeling…I don't know…I just had to come back and check if—

REGINA: I'm glad you did. I want to tell you. Remember my dream, about the bulbs?

KATE: The one in which you wanted me to be perfect?

REGINA: Kate, I'm the bulb. I'm the dark, gnarly little thing in the earth that needs to come back perfect. Not you. Me. It's me who needs to do it again.

KATE: I doubt any of us do it right.

REGINA: Kate, I want you to know…well, sometimes we must do things…sometimes it's best if—

KATE: Regina, you promised.

REGINA: Kate…I want to tell you I…I feel…I feel sorry…I regret…my weakness.

KATE: You've always been a good woman. A good wife…a good mother.

REGINA: No, no, Kate. Please, no lies. Not now. I confess, Kate…I haven't been so good. Forgive me. I let you down…in every way.

KATE: Regina…please.

KATE touches the earrings she gave to REGINA.

REGINA: I'm not saying I regret that—

KATE: You regret me?

REGINA: No, no, Kate. Lord no. I love you. Oh, my darling, Katherine, I love you more than life itself.

KATE: Never enough to give up drinking. I shouldn't have said that.

REGINA: Forgive me, Katie. Forgive me?

KATE: Regina.

REGINA: Time for you to go.

KATE: No, Regina. I want to be…with you…I want—

REGINA: Kate, listen to me. My life, it's been a small life, a little life. When I look back, I don't see very much, but I take responsibility for that. And now…and now I take responsibility for the rest of my life. I've never been particularly strong…or…or independent. But…for the first time, Kate, maybe in my entire seventy-umty-ump years, I'm taking control.

KATE: I won't let you go.

KATE's back is turned. REGINA reaches out to her.

REGINA: Letting go is what living is all about. Kate. Could you…just once…could you…call me mommy?

KATE turns around. REGINA pulls her hand back.

KATE: Regina, I…I—

REGINA: I know I don't deserve—

Pain overtakes REGINA. KATE helps her with a spoonful of morphine.

SPIRIT: Not too much.

The pain eases.

REGINA: Kate, there must be…I mean I hope…that…there must be a God. You know, some sort of organizing force, a designer.

KATE: Coco Chanel.

REGINA whirls with glee.

REGINA: Maybe, Coco Chanel. Maybe it doesn't matter.

KATE: Stop this. Stop, Regina.

REGINA: I'm fine, Kate. Really.

KATE reaches for her mother, but REGINA pushes her hands away.

REGINA: Finally I have the strength, the confidence to reach out and do what is right. You want to know why? Because I'm free.

SPIRIT: Lord, the delusions we dredge up at our deaths are worse then the ones we hold on to during our lives.

REGINA: Go home, Katie. I know your mother sounds like she's gone around the bend, but I'm just fine. The will's in the metal box. The key's over there on the table. I'm not leaving you much.

KATE: Regina.

REGINA: I never got round to writing an eulogy. Just don't let anyone lie about me.

KATE: Please, we can find a doctor—

REGINA: No.

KATE: Maybe there'll be a breakthrough drug that you can—

REGINA: Go. Go. Now.

KATE: I…I want to say. I want to say, that even though things have been hard…difficult…for us, I mean between us, I've got to say. (*Beat*) I've got to say I admire your…your grit. You've always had grit, Regina.

REGINA: Shhhh, Katie, don't.

KATE: And. And I want you to know. I don't know if…I want you to know…I…I love you. I love you and I'll…can't believe I'm saying this.

> *REGINA touches KATE's cheek.*

KATE: If anything happened to you…I'd miss you.

REGINA: Nothing's going to happen to me. Not for a while, at least. Run along, my darling. I must admit, I'm tired.

KATE: Promise me, Regina.

REGINA: Yes.

KATE: Promise me you won't—

REGINA: Kate, I'm going to take a nap. It's late. (*Looks at her watch*) Lord, it's early. You have to work tomorrow. Kate when are you going to quit that job and—

KATE: Regina.

REGINA: Sorry. Worrying about you is one of my habits.

KATE: Living is a habit, one that shouldn't be broken.

REGINA: True, true.

> *REGINA lies down on the couch. KATE covers her with the throw blanket. She leans down and kisses her mother.*

KATE: Now I lay me down to sleep—

REGINA: I pray the lord my soul to keep—

KATE: And if I should die before I wake—

REGINA: I pray the lord my soul to take.

KATE: Sleep well.

> *REGINA closes her eyes and KATE tiptoes toward the door, but quietly comes back and curls up in the overstuffed chair and goes to sleep.*
>
> *REGINA sits up, whispers.*

REGINA: Where are you? Are you ready?

SPIRIT: No.

REGINA: If not now, when?

SPIRIT: We didn't go on a wing-ding.

REGINA: We're going on one now.

REGINA takes slug of bourbon, toasts SPIRIT and then takes a slug of morphine.

REGINA: Promise me. No more distractions.

SPIRIT is silent.

REGINA: Queenie.

SPIRIT: All right.

REGINA: No more cajoling, convincing.

SPIRIT: No more.

REGINA: Sorry I've been so boring and mundane.

SPIRIT: Things have picked up recently.

REGINA: Yes, well, that's what a little terminal kick in the fanny will do for you. All right, Queenie…have we done everything? Canceled the newspaper?

SPIRIT: Check. For the third time.

REGINA: Reviewed the will, finished the puzzle?

SPIRIT: Check, check.

REGINA: We're clear on music, dress, make-up?

SPIRIT: Check, check, check.

REGINA: Oh, yes. After the memorial. I want good bourbon served. Not the cheapy stuff I usually drink. Okay, let's get on with it.

SPIRIT: Wait. Hold the phone, darling.

SPIRIT whirls to dash off stage.

REGINA: Don't call me darling.

SPIRIT returns loaded with suitcases, duffel bags, a pile of hats on her head.

REGINA: I swear woman. Don't you understand what we're about to do?

SPIRIT: (*Giggles*) We're going through the door.

REGINA: Right. Not on an ocean cruise.

SPIRIT: You don't know.

REGINA: My intuition tells me to travel light.

SPIRIT: Well, darling, I'm going prepared.

REGINA gathers duffels and suitcases.

REGINA: Queenie, where's your crown?

SPIRIT: Oh, that old thing?

REGINA: Yes, that old thing.

SPIRIT: Maybe…maybe over there I'll get a real one.

REGINA: Hope you do.

REGINA turns to show off her dress.

REGINA: How do I look?

SPIRIT pinches REGINA's cheeks, fusses with her hair.

SPIRIT: A dead ringer for a glamour puss.

REGINA: We sure are taking a lot of baggage.

SPIRIT: Everybody does.

REGINA: Well, not me.

REGINA sheds the bags.

REGINA: Ready?

SPIRIT: Yes, just about. Passport. Visas. I'm ready. Oh, Regina, you never answered me. Do you like the dress?

REGINA: It's to die for.

SPIRIT: Happy Birthday, old girl.

REGINA: Happy Birthday.

SPIRIT sings, "Where ever you go, what ever you do…" REGINA joins in. The two sing and dance wildly, they hook arms in a crazy dosie-doe. Finally the frivolity comes to an end.

REGINA moves toward the door, then she stops and makes a swooping bow indicating for SPIRIT to go through first.

SPIRIT: After you.

REGINA: No, after you.

SPIRIT: I insist.

REGINA: You first.

SPIRIT: Be my guest.

REGINA: Get your body over there.

SPIRIT: You are a difficult woman.

REGINA: Aren't we just. (*Beat*) Okay, okay, but can I trust you to follow? It's no good, you know, if you do this part way.

SPIRIT: I'll follow. Cross my heart hope to…to die.

> *REGINA throws a kiss to SPIRIT who catches it and holds her hand against her cheek. Then REGINA goes to the door.*

SPIRIT: Regina. (*REGINA stops in her tracks.*) Isn't there something profound you want to say to me?

> *REGINA takes a big breath and then looks out for a long moment.*

REGINA: Always wear clean underwear.

> *REGINA steps through the door.*
>
> *SPIRIT nervously sings "Together" as she loads herself up with bags.*

SPIRIT: Where ever we go, what ever we do, we're gonna go through it together. We may not go far, but sure as a star, what ever we are, it's together…

> *SPIRIT makes a decision. She drops the baggage. Then she moves very close to the door, tentatively peeks through.*

SPIRIT: Where ever I go, I know she goes, where ever she goes, I know I go, no fits, no fights, no feuds, no egos…amigos…together…

> *Long beat. Her singing grows quieter and quieter.*

SPIRIT: Through thick and through thin, all out and all in, and whether it's win, place or show, if you're for me, and me for you, we're not all through, whatever we do—

> *A vulnerable SPIRIT looks back, throws a kiss. She turns and determinedly goes through the door. She boldly sings, but once she passes through the door, her song is cut in mid-line.*

SPIRIT: Together, where ev—

> *Beat. KATE suddenly awakens.*

KATE: Mommy?

BLACKOUT

CURTAIN

About the Playwright

Elizabeth Appell is a playwright, screenwriter and novelist. Her full-length plays have been given directed readings in New York, Los Angeles, and San Francisco. Before it found a home at the EXIT Theatre in San Francisco, *Confessions of a Catholic Child* was produced by The Virtual Theatre Project in Los Angeles.

Appell's play *Moon Walkers* placed in several competitions including as finalist in the O'Neil. Jamie Denton (*Desperate Housewives*) took on the lead in a staged reading in Los Angeles.

Appell has written award winning short stories and several have been published. Her novel, *Lessons from the Gypsy Camp*, received rave reviews (See Amazon.com.) Her screen adaptation of the novel won several competitions and was optioned.

Appell's two short films, *Easy Made Hard* and *Warnings from the Bathtub*, were official selections at over 30 festivals and were awarded Gold in Houston. *Easy Made Hard* was screened at the Cannes Short Film Corner.

MORE PLAYS FROM EXIT PRESS

Woyzeck, Pelleas and Melisande, Ubu Roi: translated by Rob Melrose

"Rob Melrose is a kind of magician, and his theater, Cutting Ball, is one of the most exciting and integrity-filled enterprises going in the sometimes-shabby field of the American theater. These translations, lucid and sharp, are a beautiful testimony to the value of Rob's achievement." — Oskar Eustis

Three Plays by Mark Jackson

"Playwright/director Mark Jackson has made his name as a first-class theatrical provocateur. Gutsy showmanship, brainy literary instincts and laser-sharp satire mark his canon." — San Jose Mercury News This collection of plays by Mark Jackson includes three plays based on incredible historic events: *God's Plot*, *Mary Stuart*, and *Salomania*.

Songs of Hestia: Plays From the 2010 San Francisco Olympians Festival

Playwrights Nirmala Nataraj, Bennett Fisher, Stuart Eugene Bousel, Claire Rice, and Evelyn Jean Pine adapt some of Western culture's oldest stories, illuminating our present-day concerns with imagination, creativity, curiosity and passion.

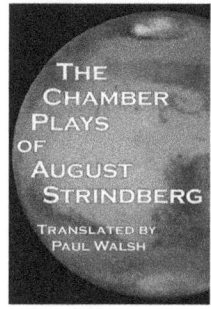

The Chamber Plays of August Strindberg translated by Paul Walsh

The Ghost Sonata, *The Pelican*, *The Black Glove*, *Storm*, and *Burned House*. Yale professor Paul Walsh provides modern translations while keeping Strindberg's "curiosity and his strangeness as specific and opaque as they are in the Swedish."

EXIT Press is the publishing division of EXIT Theatre, a San Francisco theater company founded in 1983. EXIT Press is distributed by Small Press Distribution of Berkeley, California. www.exitpress.org

www.ingramcontent.com/pod-product-compliance
Lightning Source LLC
Chambersburg PA
CBHW051705090426
42736CB00013B/2552